PRIMARY SOURCE
EXPLORERS

A JOURNEY WITH CHRISTOPHER COLUMBUS

STUART A. KALLEN

LERNER PUBLICATIONS ◆ MINNEAPOLIS

Content consultant:
Jeane DeLaney, Associate Professor of History, St. Olaf College

Lerner Publications Company
A division of Lerner Publishing Group, Inc.
241 First Avenue North
Minneapolis, MN 55401 USA

For reading levels and more information, look up this title at www.lernerbooks.com.

Main body text set in AvenirLTPro 12/18.
Typeface provided by Linotype AG.

Library of Congress Cataloging-in-Publication Data

Names: Kallen, Stuart A., 1955–
Title: A journey with Christopher Columbus / Stuart A. Kallen.
Description: Minneapolis : Lerner Publications, [2017] | Series: Primary
   source explorers | Includes bibliographical references and index. |
   Audience: Grades 4–6.
Identifiers: LCCN 2015043014 | ISBN 9781512407723 (library binding : alk.
   paper)
Subjects: LCSH: Columbus, Christopher—Juvenile literature. |
   Explorers—America—Biography—Juvenile literature. | Explorers—
   Spain—Biography—Juvenile literature. | America—Discovery and
   exploration—Spanish—Juvenile literature.
Classification: LCC E111 .K17 2017 | DDC 970.01/5092—dc23

LC record available at http://lccn.loc.gov/2015043014

Manufactured in the United States of America
1-39344-21156-9/20/2016

CONTENTS

= Denotes primary source

INTRODUCTION
THE OLD WORLD MEETS THE NEW

The Italian explorer Christopher Columbus first landed on a Caribbean island on October 12, 1492. A few days later, Columbus made an entry in his journal. He said he was searching for a village "where our Indians inform us we shall find . . . much gold."

Columbus's journal about his voyage to the New World is known as a primary source. Primary sources are documents and objects that make up the raw materials of history. Other primary sources from Columbus's era include drawings and paintings, tools, trade goods, clothing, and diaries written by people who lived at the same time as Columbus.

Columbus wrote this letter in November 1493 to describe his second voyage to the New World. Because we can read his words, we know what he saw and thought hundreds of years ago, even though he can't tell us in person.

Columbus's original journal, in which he described his experience exploring the New World, no longer exists. But another colonist, Bartolomé de Las Casas, wrote his own version of the events. That text (pictured) includes direct quotations and summaries of Columbus's words. That history is the version of Columbus's words that modern scholars use.

The value of primary sources can be seen in the sentence Columbus wrote in his journal. He called the Native people Indians because he believed he was in India. Columbus never knew Hispaniola (modern Dominican Republic and Haiti) is in the Caribbean Sea, thousands of miles from India.

When Columbus mentions gold, he reveals an important reason for his journey. Columbus was driven by dreams of wealth and power. During the four voyages Columbus made to the New World between 1492 and 1504, his goals were finding gold and spreading his religious views.

Although Columbus visited the New World more than five hundred years ago, his journal opens a window on his journeys. Taken together, the primary sources of the era provide a snapshot of a distant time. After people of the Old World came face-to-face with those of the new, neither world would ever be the same.

This sixteenth-century painting shows the harbor of Genoa, Italy, where Columbus was born. By the time this art was created, the age of exploration was well under way. This painting is not considered a primary source, because it was not made at the time of the event.

CHAPTER 1
THE DREAMS OF AN EXPLORER

Christopher Columbus was born in 1451 in Genoa, Italy. Genoa was a port city on the Mediterranean Ocean where ocean exploration was a way of life. Explorers regularly sailed from Genoa to a chain of islands called the Azores, in the Atlantic Ocean west of Portugal.

SPICES, SILK, AND GEMS

Some in Genoa grew rich buying and selling goods. Traders shipped wool from England, cloth from Belgium, and glass artwork from Venice, Italy. The richest traders bought and sold spices, silk, gold, gems, and pearls. These were imported from the East—modern-day India, China, Japan, and Indonesia.

Traders of items such as silk and spices faced a problem. There was no sea route between Europe and the East. The goods were brought to Europe in camel caravans. The camels walked nose to tail along a 4,000-mile (6,437-kilometer) web of paths called the Silk Road. The route connected China and India to ports on the Mediterranean in eastern Europe.

The Silk Road was dangerous. Traders faced sandstorms in the deserts and snowstorms in the mountains. Parts of the route were controlled by bandits. Plus, in the 1450s, new leaders in eastern Europe made it even harder for western Europeans to travel the Silk Road. That inspired explorers to seek a water route to the East.

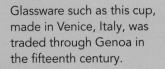

Glassware such as this cup, made in Venice, Italy, was traded through Genoa in the fifteenth century.

This world map, drawn by Paolo dal Pozzo Toscanelli, became a best seller when it was produced in 1475. Columbus knew of this map, but modern scholars disagree about whether he believed it was completely accurate.

LEARNING TO NAVIGATE

As a young man, Christopher learned geography by reading maps and charts created by explorers. He studied a navigation technique called dead reckoning, in which a sailor tracks his location by measuring the distance and direction he's traveled from his starting point. Later in life, Columbus learned to speak and write Portuguese and Spanish.

AN INEXACT MAP

Columbus went to work as a seaman on merchant ships called galleys when he was nineteen. He sailed thousands of miles on trade trips through the Mediterranean. Columbus's travels took him to Lisbon, the capital of Portugal.

Columbus spent eight years in Lisbon. He was joined there by his brother Bartholomew Columbus, who went into business selling navigational tools, books, and maps. One of the best-selling maps of the world was created by an Italian geographer named Paolo dal Pozzo Toscanelli.

The map was not accurate. It made Earth seem much smaller than it is. Toscanelli did not know that North and South America and the Pacific Ocean existed. The map wrongly showed China as west of Europe, across the Atlantic Ocean.

This view of geography helped convince Columbus he could reach the East by sailing west across the Atlantic. Fast sailing ships called carracks could sail 100 miles (161 km) a day. Columbus believed he could reach China in thirty days.

Columbus used this magnetic compass to navigate to the New World. This tool helped him determine his location and kept him on course.

REJECTED BY THE KING

In 1479 Columbus married Filipa Moniz Perestrelo, the daughter of a wealthy Portuguese nobleman. Because of her status, Columbus was able to meet João II, king of Portugal. In 1483

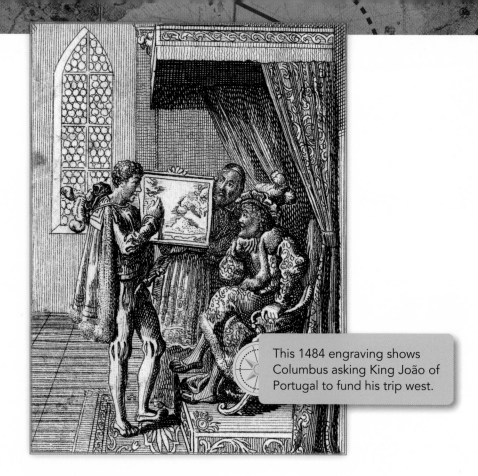

This 1484 engraving shows Columbus asking King João of Portugal to fund his trip west.

Columbus tried to convince the king to pay for a mission across the Atlantic. But the king believed the idea of sailing west to find the East was a fantasy. After being spurned, Columbus left for Spain in 1485. He would spend the next seven years trying to convince Spanish royalty to back his plans.

WHAT DO YOU THINK?

Columbus spent years asking kings to pay for his journey west. What do you think he might have said or done to try to convince them?

This 1794 engraving shows Columbus (front) with his wife (right) and two sons.

FERDINAND COLUMBUS PORTRAYS HIS FATHER

Ferdinand Columbus wrote a book about his father, Christopher Columbus, in 1536. Here, Ferdinand describes his father's appearance:

> [Columbus was a] well built man of more than medium stature, long [faced] with cheeks somewhat high, but neither fat nor thin. He had a [hooked] nose and his eyes were light in color; his complexion too was light, but kindling to a vivid red. In his youth his hair was blond but when it came to his thirtieth year it all turned white.

King Ferdinand *(left)* and Queen Isabella of Spain, as drawn in 1482, a few years before they finally agreed to pay for Columbus's trip west

CHAPTER 2
ONE-TENTH OF
ALL RICHES

In 1486 Christopher Columbus, at thirty-four, was still hoping to set up a profitable trade network with China. After a year in Spain, he convinced the Spanish king and queen to meet with him. Columbus showed King Ferdinand and Queen Isabella a map of a westward journey he wanted to take across the Atlantic Ocean to China. Columbus wanted them to pay for his voyage. The royals eventually turned Columbus down, calling his idea unworkable.

A ROYAL CONTRACT

During the next few years, Columbus explained his plans to Spain's leading scholars, clergymen, geographers, and ship

COLUMBUS'S JOURNEYS TO THE NEW WORLD

Florida

GUANAHANI (SAN SALVADOR)

BAHAMAS

ATLANTIC OCEAN

CUBA

La Isabela

La Navidad

HISPANIOLA

VIRGIN ISLANDS

SAINT KITTS

MONTSERRAT

Saint Ann's Bay

HAITI

Santo Domingo

N

JAMAICA

PUERTO RICO

SAINT CROIX

LESSER ANTILLES

CARIBBEAN SEA

Belén River

PANAMA

VENEZUELA

First journey 1492–1493
Second journey 1493–1496
Third journey 1498–1500
Fourth journey 1502–1504
Present-day country border

SOUTH AMERICA

PACIFIC OCEAN

captains. In early 1492, these powerful people convinced Ferdinand and Isabella to pay for Columbus's voyage of discovery.

On April 17, the Spanish monarchs made their support official by signing a contract in Santa Fe, Spain. The Santa Fe Capitulations granted Columbus the rank of admiral of the islands. Columbus would be made viceroy, or governor, of all new lands he claimed for Spain. And Columbus would receive one-tenth of all gold and other riches found in the new lands. If his plan succeeded, Columbus would become rich.

This modern drawing shows Columbus's ships leaving Palos, Spain, in 1492.

A LONG JOURNEY

Columbus outfitted three ships for the voyage. The *Santa María* was a large carrack, while the *Niña* and *Pinta* were smaller caravels. Caravels were about 75 feet (23 meters) long by 20 feet (6 m) wide. This small size meant that the ships were fast and easy to maneuver.

The expedition set sail from Palos, Spain, on the morning of August 3. Columbus had promised his sailors that their journey would be short. But after a few weeks at sea, there was still no land in sight. The men were growing restless. Ships on long journeys tended to be cramped. Without refrigerators, food rotted and reeked in storage barrels. There was little fresh water to drink and none to bathe in. Diseases thrived and sailors were often sickened by the flu and other ailments.

By the first week in October, there was talk of mutiny. Some of the sailors wanted to arrest Columbus and turn the ships around. Emotions changed from anger to joy on October 12. At two o'clock in the morning, a watchman shouted *"Tierra, tierra,"* the Spanish word for land. As the sun rose, the sailors could see beaches and palm trees ahead.

"VERY FRIENDLY" TAINO

Columbus and a small party of sailors took a boat to shore. Columbus planted a royal flag in the sand. The island where Columbus landed is known as San Salvador in modern times.

In the late twentieth century, artist Jean Leon Gerome Ferris painted this image of Columbus arriving on Guanahani. Ferris painted many well-known events in American history, but his artwork often depicted things incorrectly.

This modern photo shows a beach on San Salvador. It is likely that Columbus and his crew saw a similar view of the island when they landed.

But when Columbus arrived, the Taino people who lived there called the island Guanahani. Some scholars estimate that three million Taino lived on the Caribbean islands, which include Hispaniola, Haiti, the Bahamas, Cuba, Jamaica, and Puerto Rico.

The Taino had lived in the area for hundreds of years and had built a complex, self-sufficient society. They grew corn, beans, sweet potatoes, and other vegetables. They grew cotton and weaved it into cloth. The Taino invented words we still use, including *canoe*, *hammock*, *barbecue*, *tobacco*, and *hurricane*.

The Taino did not threaten the new arrivals. As Columbus wrote, "I saw that they were very friendly to us. . . . I presented them with some red caps, and strings of beads to wear upon the neck, and many other trifles of small value. . . . They were much delighted, and became wonderfully attached to us."

Scholars believe this Taino seat was used in the fourteenth or fifteenth century in Hispaniola.

A TAINO HONOR

Duho seats were made and used by Taino people around the time of Columbus's arrival. This kind of seat had special meaning to the Taino. Chiefs used duhos to communicate with the spirit world, which helped them make important decisions for the people. When Columbus arrived, the Taino honored him by allowing him to sit on a duho. Columbus saw bits of gold in the duho, which strengthened his belief that the Caribbean islands were filled with gold he could take back to Europe. In reality, the Taino had very small amounts of gold, and putting it in this seat showed how sacred the seat was to them.

Taino in the Caribbean made these stone carvings between 1000 and 1500. Scholars think they represented Taino spirits.

Columbus was relieved the Taino were peaceful. But he viewed their openness as a sign of weakness. He wrote in his journal, "I could conquer the whole of them with fifty men, and govern them as I pleased."

SEARCHING FOR GOLD

Columbus noticed some of the Taino wore gold jewelry. Columbus used hand gestures to ask the Native people where he could find gold. It is likely the Taino did not understand Columbus. But they described other islands the Europeans could explore.

Columbus and his men soon sailed to Cuba and other islands. They did not find gold. On December 6, the explorers landed on an island Columbus called Hispaniola (modern Haiti and the Dominican Republic). The Native people there had gold statues, which they gave the Europeans as gifts. At the end of December, Columbus sailed away from Hispaniola. He

COLUMBUS DESCRIBES THE TAINO

When Christopher Columbus landed on San Salvador, he met local Taino who he described in his journal:

> They all go completely naked, even the women. . . . Some paint the face [black], and some the whole body; others only [around] the eyes, and others the nose. Weapons they have none, nor are acquainted with them, for I showed them swords which they grasped by the blades, and cut themselves through ignorance. They have no iron, their javelins being without it, and nothing more than sticks, though some have fish-bones or other things at the ends.

left thirty-nine men behind to set up a colony he named La Navidad.

On January 16, 1493, Columbus began his return voyage. On March 24, Columbus dropped anchor in the harbor of Palos, Spain. After a thirty-two-week journey, he had much to celebrate. He had discovered what was later called the New World. The king and queen of Spain named Columbus viceroy and governor of the Indies.

WHAT DO YOU THINK?

What kinds of details did Columbus notice about the Taino? What does that tell you about his values?

In 1494 Spain and Portugal signed the Treaty of Tordesillas. This agreement divided the land Columbus had claimed in the New World.

CHAPTER 3
RETURNING TO THE NEW WORLD

Christopher Columbus returned to Spain in 1493 believing he had visited islands of Japan, China, or India. Within weeks he was plotting his return trip. Columbus wanted to take his position as governor of the Caribbean islands he had visited, and he wanted to convert the Native people to Christianity. Like most Europeans at the time, Columbus believed it was his duty to bring the Christian religion to the rest of the world.

SEVENTEEN SHIPS

Columbus assembled a large fleet for his second voyage. On September 24, seventeen ships holding twelve hundred men sailed from Cádiz, Spain. Columbus planned to set up a permanent colony, so his ships held farm animals. The explorers also brought wheat and sugarcane to plant.

The Spanish fleet arrived at a group of Caribbean islands called the Lesser Antilles on November 3. During the next two weeks, Columbus sailed northwest to Hispaniola. The fleet stopped at numerous beautiful islands, including Montserrat, Saint Kitts, Saint Croix, and the Virgin Islands.

This woodcut of the colony of La Isabela was published in a 1494 edition of Columbus's report on his voyage to the New World. It's unlikely that anyone on the journey actually created this image, but it was made around the same time.

When Columbus returned to La Navidad in late November, he discovered that all thirty-nine Europeans he had left behind the previous December were dead. Some had died from disease. Others were killed by a Taino chief who wished to rid the island of European intruders. Some of Columbus's men wanted to go to war with the chief, but Columbus thought it unwise. He was more interested in sailing the coastline of Hispaniola in search of a new place to build a colony.

CHAOS IN THE COLONY

In early January 1494, the Spaniards founded a colony on Hispaniola called La Isabela. The newcomers built about one hundred huts and a church. Columbus's brother Bartholomew was put in charge of the colony.

In March Columbus and four hundred men set out to search for gold. They traveled on foot across rivers, up mountains, and through forests. The explorers found parrots, pineapples, and beautiful flowers but little gold.

Columbus returned to La Isabela to act as governor. But the colony was facing problems. The Spaniards were trying to raise food, but they rarely had enough to eat. To make matters worse, many men were sick and dying. Many of them blamed Columbus for their problems. He had promised them riches, but

The ruins of La Isabela, in present-day Dominican Republic

THE SUFFERING OF THE TAINO

Columbus has long been criticized for the way he treated the Taino. As governor of Hispaniola, Columbus ordered his men to kidnap about sixteen hundred Taino. Some were forced to search the island for gold. Others were used as farm slaves. Five hundred Taino were shipped back to Europe and sold as slaves.

European diseases also took their toll. After Columbus arrived, about one-third of the Taino died from smallpox, measles, and other ailments. To escape, unknown numbers fled to regions beyond colonial control. Many historians believe that by 1520, the original Taino population had been reduced by as much as 85 percent.

instead, they had found suffering and death. When several men spoke of mutiny, Columbus had them whipped and hanged.

THE THIRD VOYAGE

In March 1496, Columbus sailed back to Spain with 225 Europeans, a few Native people, and very little gold. He left orders with Bartholomew to build a new capital called Santo Domingo on the southern coast of Hispaniola.

For the next twenty months, Columbus prepared for his third voyage to the New World. He was forty-six when he set out again for Hispaniola on May 30, 1498. By then Ferdinand and Isabella were growing tired of paying for Columbus's journeys. On his third voyage, Columbus was only given a fleet of six ships, about a third as many as for his previous journey.

This nineteenth-century painting shows explorer Alonso de Ojeda encouraging Hispaniola colonists to revolt against Columbus. Ojeda wanted the same power and riches Columbus was seeking.

PUTTING DOWN A REVOLT

By the time Columbus reached Hispaniola, he was in poor health. He had an eye infection and was suffering from what he thought was gout, which made walking difficult. Columbus was in no shape to govern and hoped to rest. Instead, he found himself in the middle of a revolution.

The Hispaniola colonists had divided into two factions. One group loyal to Bartholomew controlled the central and southern parts of the island. A second group had appointed its own viceroy and moved to an isolated region. When Columbus arrived, he ended the revolution with violence. He tortured and hanged dozens of rebels.

IRON SHACKLES

Columbus also had problems in Spain. Some men who had been on the second voyage told the king and queen that Columbus was a brutal and unjust ruler. One report said Columbus had cut off the ears and nose of a man accused of stealing corn. When Columbus killed Native people, the story went on, their bodies were dragged through the streets as a warning.

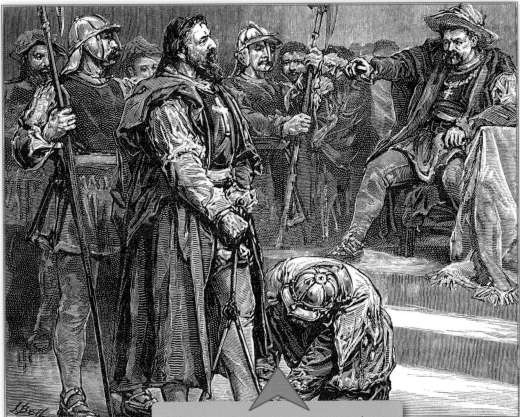

This nineteenth-century engraving shows Columbus being arrested for treating people poorly in the New World.

During an excavation at La Isabela, archaeologists found huge amounts of pottery *(right)*. Most of it had been made and used by Europeans, but some had belonged to Native people.

DIGGING FOR PRIMARY SOURCES

La Isabela was an active colony for only four or five years, from about 1493 to 1497. About fifteen hundred European men lived there during that time. In the 1980s and 1990s, archaeologists from the Dominican National Park Service, the National Experimental University "Francisco de Miranda" in Venezuela, and the University of Florida researched and excavated the site of the colony. Many of the artifacts they found, which can be considered primary sources, were later put on display in Dominican Republic museums.

Archaeologists use the primary sources found at the site to understand what life was like in the colony. They used these artifacts, along with the written documentation of the colony that still exists, to put together a portrait of the time and place.

The king and queen decided to end Columbus's rule. They sent a nobleman named Francisco de Bobadilla to remove Columbus from power. Bobadilla arrived in Santo Domingo on August 24, 1500, and arrested Columbus. The admiral of the islands was sent back to Spain in iron shackles. For Columbus it was a crushing end to a disastrous voyage.

WHAT DO YOU THINK?

Why do you think Columbus was accused of being a bad governor? How did his attitudes toward Native people influence his governing style?

CHAPTER 4
THE HIGH VOYAGE

Christopher Columbus was arrested and returned to Spain in 1500. But King Ferdinand and Queen Isabella set Columbus free after only six weeks. The Spanish rulers still needed the skills of an expert explorer.

The king and queen feared rivals in Portugal would establish trade routes to India, which would weaken the Spanish economy. And they had reason to worry. In 1499 Portuguese explorer Vasco da Gama found a sea route to India by sailing around the southern tip of Africa. In March 1502, Ferdinand and Isabella sponsored a fourth journey for Columbus. Columbus had grand plans. He told the king and queen he would find the Strait of

Malacca. Columbus had read that this water passage led to the Indian Ocean. But the Strait of Malacca is between Malaysia and Singapore in Southeast Asia. Columbus believed it was in the islands he'd visited, which he wrongly thought were in Asia.

SEARCHING FOR A STRAIT

Columbus set out from Spain on May 11, 1502. The crew included Columbus's thirteen-year-old son Ferdinand. The journey started out well. Columbus crossed the Atlantic in record time.

After reaching the Caribbean, Columbus's fleet sailed down the coast of Central America. The ships arrived in present-day Honduras at the end of July. For the next two months, Columbus explored the Central American coastline. He was searching for a body of water that might lead to the Strait of Malacca.

Jungle on the coast of Panama

This sixteenth-century tapestry shows Vasco de Gama arriving in Calicut, India.

VASCO DA GAMA REACHES INDIA

Portuguese explorer Vasco da Gama was the first European to find a sea route to India. In July 1497, da Gama led four ships south of Lisbon along the coast of Africa. The fleet reached the southern tip of Africa at the Cape of Good Hope in December and headed northeast. Da Gama's fleet arrived in Calicut, India, in May 1498.

Da Gama's return home was a disaster. By the time his ships reached the Cape of Good Hope in early 1499, half his crew had died of disease or starvation. Da Gama and the surviving sailors finally made it back to Lisbon in late July.

When Columbus arrived in Panama in October, his hopes were raised. The Native people there told him about another sea that lay to the west. People were referring to the Pacific Ocean. The locals said it could be reached by marching overland for a few days. In Panama a strip of dense jungle about 50 miles (80 km) wide separates the Pacific Ocean from the Atlantic.

This gold disc was made in Panama sometime between 300 and 1550. The people Columbus encountered in Panama may have worn jewelry similar to this.

But Columbus was not interested in hiking overland. The information about the sea fulfilled his belief that he was close to the Strait of Malacca. With this settled in his mind, Columbus returned to his quest for gold. Native people in the region wore round, gold objects around their necks. These were freely given to the explorers or traded for little bells.

The gold jewelry convinced Columbus he had finally found a rich source of gold, ten years after his first voyage to the region. He set up a gold mining colony on the Belén River in Panama. But the colony did not last. The Native people had been treated poorly by other Europeans. They didn't trust the new colonists. The Native people attacked the European explorers, and a battle left many dead on both sides.

STRANDED

On April 16, 1503, the surviving sailors left Panama. Columbus was eager to return to Spain to tell the king and queen he had discovered gold. But Columbus was in trouble. His ships were falling apart. They were battered from storms and covered with mollusks called shipworms, which eat holes in wood. Columbus described the efforts of his men to keep their ship from sinking: "[With] the use of pots and kettles, we could scarcely . . . clear the water that came into the ship, there being no remedy but this for the mischief done by the ship-worm."

With his ships unable to stay afloat, Columbus made an emergency landing in Jamaica in June. The Europeans were stranded for a year on Saint Ann's Bay. To avoid war with the Native people who lived there, Columbus made a deal. His men would remain on their leaky ships if the locals brought them food.

This engraving shows Columbus in Jamaica around 1504. The engraving was made in the sixteenth century by a German artist, who did not witness the event. Artists used journals and letters from explorers, but they often misrepresented people and events, especially Native peoples.

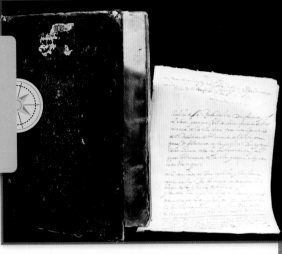

In 1502 Columbus collected all the royal documents he'd received about his trips and had them officially signed and notarized. Together, these are called his *Book of Privileges*. This paperwork also confirmed that Spain owned the land Columbus had claimed and could send more explorers in the future.

Columbus sent one of his men to Hispaniola in a canoe to ask for help. Fresh ships and supplies finally arrived in Jamaica in late June 1504. Columbus and his surviving crew landed in Spain on November 7.

DEATH OF AN EXPLORER

Three weeks after Columbus returned to Spain, Queen Isabella died. Columbus himself was often so sick he could barely leave his bed. He used what energy he had to write letters to King Ferdinand. Columbus wanted the 10 percent of New World profits he had been promised in 1492. But without the queen's support, the king had little interest in paying Columbus.

Columbus died in Valladolid, Spain, on May 20, 1506, at the age of fifty-four. Had he lived longer, he would have learned of the existence of North and South America. But Columbus remained convinced he had sailed to the outskirts of India. And he continued to believe that riches lay just over the horizon.

WHAT DO YOU THINK?

Why do you think King Ferdinand was reluctant to pay Columbus? Do you think nonpayment was fair for either the king or for Columbus?

TIMELINE

1451 Christopher Columbus is born in Genoa, Italy.

1476 Columbus moves to Lisbon, Portugal.

1479 Columbus marries Filipa Moniz Perestrelo, the daughter of a wealthy nobleman.

1484 The king of Portugal refuses to back Columbus's plan to find a sea route to Asia.

1492 In August, with the financial backing of King Ferdinand and Queen Isabella of Spain, Columbus sets sail for the New World.

1493 Columbus returns to Spain for a few months, then departs on his second voyage to the New World.

1496 Columbus returns to Spain once again.

1498 Columbus sets sail on his third voyage to the New World.

1500 Columbus is arrested in Hispaniola for poor governing and sent back to Spain in chains.

1502 Columbus makes his fourth and final voyage, which takes him to Central America.

1504 Columbus returns home to Spain.

1506 On May 20, Columbus dies in Spain at the age of fifty-four.

SOURCE NOTES

4   Christopher Columbus, *Personal Narrative of the First Voyage* (Boston: Thomas B. Wait and Son, 1827), 54.

11   Ferdinand Columbus, quoted in Laurence Bergreen, *Columbus: The Four Voyages* (New York: Viking, 2011), 61.

14   "Christopher Columbus," *Explorers & Discoverers of the World* (Detroit: Gale, 1993), *Biography in Context*. http://sproxy .glenbrook225.org/login?url=http://ic.galegroup.com/ic/bic1 /ReferenceDetailsPage/ReferenceDetailsWindow?query=&prodId =BIC1&displayGroupName=Reference&limiter=&disable Highlighting=true&displayGroups=&sortBy=&zid=&search _within_results=&action=2&catId=GALE%7C00000000MR3T&activity Type=&documentId=GALE%7CK1614000078&userGroupName =gotitans&source=Bookmark&u=gotitans&jsid=c38ce7b5b8a1921f 1ecd91de8f01fa22. 29 July 2016.

16   Columbus, *Personal Narrative*, 35.

18   Ibid., 40.

19   Ibid., 35–36.

32   Christopher Columbus, *Select Letters of Christopher Columbus, with Other Original Documents*, ed. Richard Henry Major (New York: Cambridge University Press, 2010), 195.

GLOSSARY

capitulation: a set of the terms of an agreement, or conditions

carrack: a large merchant ship that was fast and easy to maneuver

expedition: a journey, or voyage, undertaken by a group of people with a specific purpose

galley: a type of low, flat ship with one or more sails and up to three banks of oars, mainly used for trade and warfare

mutiny: open rebellion by sailors or soldiers against their officers

New World: the Western Hemisphere, including North and South America

Old World: Europe

strait: a narrow passage of water that connects two seas

SELECTED BIBLIOGRAPHY

Bergreen, Laurence. *Columbus: The Four Voyages.* New York: Viking, 2011.

Columbus, Christopher. *Personal Narrative of the First Voyage.* Boston: Thomas B. Wait and Son, 1827.

Deagan, Kathleen A. *Columbus's Outpost among the Taínos: Spain and America at La Isabela, 1493–1498.* New Haven, CT: Yale University Press, 2002.

Dugard, Martin. *The Last Voyage of Columbus: Being the Epic Tale of the Great Captain's Fourth Expedition, Including Accounts of Mutiny, Shipwreck, and Discovery.* New York: Back Bay Books, 2006.

Sale, Kirkpatrick. *Christopher Columbus and the Conquest of Paradise.* New York: Tauris Parke Paperbacks, 2006.

FURTHER INFORMATION

Allen, Kathy. *When Did Columbus Arrive in the Americas? And Other Questions about Columbus's Voyages.* Minneapolis: Lerner Publications, 2012. Learn more about why Columbus traveled west to the Americas and the challenges he and his crew faced along the way.

Berne, Emma Carlson. *Did Christopher Columbus Really Discover America? And Other Questions about the New World.* New York: Sterling Children's Books, 2014. This book shines a light on the Taino people who lived on the islands Columbus visited.

Christopher Columbus
http://www.history.com/topics/exploration/christopher-columbus
This site features information about Columbus's life, videos about his ships and crew, and related content about other explorers.

Landau, Elaine. *Discovering a New World: Would You Sail with Columbus?* Berkeley Heights, NJ: Enslow Elementary, 2015. This book invites the reader to travel along on Columbus's voyages. Would you go along with all of Columbus's decisions?

Pre-Columbian Hispaniola—Arawak/Taino Indians
http://www.hartford-hwp.com/archives/43a/100.html
This site focuses on the Native peoples of the Caribbean and their homes, food, defense, religion, and leaders.

INDEX

PHOTO ACKNOWLEDGMENTS